T0355006

# HOLD
## THE
## DARKNESS
### CLOSE

by R. Gordon Zyne

Novels
Degrees of Desire
Shiners
Malchus One Ear


Poetry and Spiritual Writings
Messiah Works
Meditations on the Ultimate Concern
The Eternal Source
Spirit Care


Art and Creative Design
RichardGordonZyne.com

# HOLD
# THE
# DARKNESS
# CLOSE

THEOPOETIC
HAIKU AND SENRYU
POETRY

## R. GORDON ZYNE

# HOLD THE DARKNESS CLOSE
## THEOPOETIC HAIKU AND SENRYU POETRY

*iUniverse books may be ordered through booksellers or by contacting:*

*iUniverse*
*1663 Liberty Drive*
*Bloomington, IN 47403*
*www.iuniverse.com*
*844-349-9409*

*Cover Art by R. Gordon Zyne*

*ISBN: 978-1-6632-6835-8 (sc)*
*ISBN: 978-1-6632-6836-5 (e)*

*Library of Congress Control Number: 2024922846*

*Print information available on the last page.*

*iUniverse rev. date: 10/24/2024*

For

Paula

Danny, Nick, Jessica

Maddie and Tuna

and

All the Lovers of Life and Living Things on the Earth

# Introduction

A theopoetic haiku or senryu is a fusion of poetry and spirituality, using the traditional 5-7-5 haiku form to explore human experiences, divine insights, and the connection between the sacred and everyday life. Its simplicity distills complex emotions into brief, evocative lines that resonate deeply. While haiku traditionally focuses on nature and seasons, senryu, a related form, emphasizes human nature, humor, and irony. Both haiku and theopoetics, though distinct, share a profound ability to evoke the divine and human experience through minimal yet powerful language, embracing paradoxes of life and faith.

Both forms invite the reader to see beyond the surface of words and into the deeper realities they point toward, whether through meditative reflection or humor.

1

grasping it slips free
change flows like untamed currents
carrying me on

2

shifting like shadows
yet rooted in the still depths
existence flows on

3

eyes fixed on bright skies
with faith in mercy I stride
unburdened by fear

4

reaching through the void
a fragile thread pulls us back
into shared struggle

5

in stillness grace breathes
sins dissolve like morning mist
soul finds quiet rest

6

in stillness peace flows
the world loosens its tight grip
with just enough joy

7

crawling through alleys
searching for love in the dark
corners of myself

8

each breath a question
each sigh a prayer to nowhere
cast into the night

9

the road twists deeper
gutters of my soul winding
where old griefs gather

10

shadows dance with light
silent sentinels of loss
watch my spirit bow

11

I thought I'd find you
in the bright fields of morning
but you hide in dust


12

in forgotten dreams
whispering through empty streets
where hope clings to pain


13

here light meets shadow
where brokenness still believes
it can find a way


14

in this darkened place
I trace the shape of absence
with a blind man's touch


15

I know you are near
a soft glow at the edge of
despair's quiet song

16

not blinding with light
but a whisper in the wound
a gentle presence

17

in the quiet place
where shadow and soul embrace
your love fills the air

18

cradling the heart
where the broken meets Divine
and loss is embraced

19

in the beginning
God spoke into the silence
form rose from formless

20

light parted from dark
day from night shadows fled far
and it was good then

21

sky stretched overhead
waters gathered below land
earth rose to greet them


22

land brought forth new life
trees plants seeds all in due time
earth green with promise


23

sun ruled the bright day
moon guarded the quiet night
stars marked time's rhythm


24

waters teemed with life
birds soared across endless skies
motion filled the world


25

beasts walked upon land
wild and free each in its kind
breathing earth's great song

26

then God breathed deep love
humankind rose in Her image
male and female called


27

to live and to care
to be in Divine likeness
bearing light and grace


28

world in its fullness
God saw and knew it was good
very good indeed


29

evening to morning
creation's quiet song rose
echoing pure joy


30

eyes fixed on the light
horizon of hope ahead
I walk forth with faith

31

God's mercy my strength
burdened not beyond my will
each step grace alone

32

cracked sidewalks unfold
past broken bottles and ash
lost souls haunt bar stools

33

faith a strange old coat
found just when you need it most
wraps you in its warmth

34

I keep moving on
trusting in the unseen truth
one step at a time

35

knowing this weight held
won't shatter or break my back
it bends but won't snap

36

in quiet night hours
when the city finally sleeps
I feel that soft lift

37

Divine grace unseen
lifting me pushing me on
reminding me here

38

I am not alone
even when shadows close in
light whispers through cracks

39

faith gripped like a bone
my anchor in rough sea waves
crash and howl around

40

patience walks with me
old friend through rain and grime's weight
bars and broken dreams

41

trouble's storm rages
world spins wild out of control
I cast fear aside


42

God guides my lost heart
a compass in the chaos
points me to stillness


43

I find my own way
stumbling yet always forward
reaching for the light


44

a dawn's promise breaks
through a city's shadowed streets
faint light where hope clings


45

in the theater's glare
lights too bright air too cold sharp
we lay bare and bleed

46

walls press in around
machines hum their empty song
life and death entwine

47

gloved hands reach and pull
nurses with eyes worn and dim
tend to what remains

48

in the end just us
facing the endless silence
no applause no sound

49

we came in with hope
left with only fading breaths
where dreams turn to dust

50

truth slices deeper
than any surgeon's clean cut
leaving us undone

51

to cross this abyss
where shadows stretch long and thin
chasm yawns open

52

we map inner worlds
chart unknown with trembling trust
and bare vulnerability

53

a tightrope journey
no safety net waiting there
just hearts on the line

54

needs of love held tight
clinging like drunks at last call
fragile hands grasping

55

teaching and learning
we stumble through the darkness
igniting hope's flame

56

each step a promise
honesty lighting our way
through fear's heavy mist


57

courage to walk blind
lay ourselves bare in the night
and discover light


58

we are not alone
our hearts reach out through the void
holding onto hope


59

in love's wide terrain
chasm stretches deep and far
emptiness resounds


60

minds search for a bridge
something strong to span the gap
understanding's path

61

lost in turbulence
where words fumble and falter
but trust threads the link

62

hearts reach and relearn
like old friends meeting anew
after years apart

63

stumbling through the dark
grasping for that thin connection
fragile thread of hope

64

pulling from the edge
of loneliness' cold grasp
back into the warmth

65

the struggle to blend
two souls in a dance of one
chaotic and pure

66

finding deep meaning
in the spaces where words fail
love's whisper abides


67

your eyes dissect me
cut me into tiny bits
spread on cold steel trays


68

always probing deep
those soft spots beneath the skin
underbelly bare


69

dragging across rocks
sharp edges tear through the flesh
leaving open wounds


70

suction and suture
sealing what cannot be healed
still the blood runs free

71

we both lie broken
under indifferent lights
in that sterile room

72

it's a brutal dance
autopsy of what once was
love cut open wide

73

we lay ourselves bare
seeking some form of rescue
some faint absolution

74

glass shatters like hope
fractured dreams of the forgotten
night weaves its dark web

75

in the bar's furnace
last call rings a desperate plea
city drinks to forget

76

neon lights flicker
broken halos cast on souls
lost lonely damned ones

77

smoke curls in silence
mixes with murmurs of pain
and laughter gone mad

78

glasses clink like bells
distant echoes of regret
tied to empty years

79

bartender a ghost
polishes worn down counters
eyes heavy with tales

80

thousand stories pass
joy and sorrow in brief waves
he stays unmoving

81

in the far corner
a woman with dreamless eyes
sips whiskey and sighs

82

unspoken anguish
something lost or someone gone
drowned in amber glass

83

man hunched over beer
stares deep into foamy depths
as if it holds truth

84

hands tremble lips shake
remembers when hope was real
now he drinks to fade

85

jukebox sings softly
melancholy notes drift out
for the broken hearts

86

music seeps through cracks
into crevices of souls
tapestry of loss

87

outside the streets hum
a chaotic dance of lights
shadows laugh and cry

88

the sea whispers low
tales of time's unending flow
lullaby for pain

89

in the bar's dark cage
the souls gather seeking peace
connection unnamed

90

they drink to forget
to remember to feel numb
escape crushing weight

91

bartender calls out
last call a final sad note
souls drift into night

92

city breathes in time
with the sea with the bar's hum
fragile fleeting world

93

glass shatters again
night weaves a new tapestry
of joy grief and dreams

94

and the world spins on
in its endless tragic dance
beautiful and raw

95

mad men wander lost
streets filled with shadows of dreams
broken by the fight

96

devils in orange shades
hollow eyes and trembling hands
beg for forgiveness

97

clothes hang on thin frames
faces etched with lines of sin
thousand regrets deep

98

redemption they seek
in bottom of empty glass
in neon's false glow

99

forgiveness a ghost
mocking them from just beyond
always out of reach

100

Jesus takes a sip
storm thickens above the bar
air heavy with grief

101

patrons glance his way
curious indifferent
something familiar

102

he's the lost savior
bearing burdens sharing pain
broken like the rest

103

bartender stands still
silent witness in the storm
steady hands pour drinks

104

city outside hums
symphony of sirens wails
shouts mix with whispers

105

mad men dance through night
macabre ballet of hope
desperation's waltz

106

neon lights reflect
in their empty hollow eyes
false promises gleam

107

hands reach out for more
something to fill the deep void
silence screaming loud

108

Jesus sees it all
labyrinth of broken dreams
mosaic of pain

109

storm gathers its force
barroom air thickens with weight
dark cloud hangs above

110

patrons drown their pain
rituals of escape made
numb to all but drink

111

mad men roam the streets
footsteps echo through the night
city's hollow heart

112

begging for reprieve
from the endless march of time
suffering's cruel loop

113

forgiveness slips past
fleeting shadow in dim light
bitter taste remains

114

Jesus breathes it in
eyes closed like a silent prayer
storm breaks with a roar

115

rain washes away
sins sorrows and shattered dreams
city cleansed anew

116

mad men stand in rain
faces lifted to the sky
hope fills empty eyes

117

lost and found they are
damned and redeemed in one breath
shadows mix with light

118

bar's quiet again
storm rages on in the night
air thick with new hope

119

city won't give up
fighting hard against the dark
fragile thread of grace

120

broken promises
ghosts in the room's dark corners
shadows of lost words

121

spaghetti on floor
chaotic tangle of grief
testament to loss


122

anger spilled like wine
words flung sharp across the night
silence stretched too long


123

mozzarella sought
hope in a sea of red sauce
untouched by the storm


124

cracked plates tell their tale
meals shared now only echoes
laughter turned to ache


125

she stands trembling still
eyes on shattered remnants cold
a dinner meant to heal

126

he sits head in hands
thinking of words never said
gestures never made

127

love now lies scattered
wreckage of unmet dreams falls
broken on the tiles

128

spaghetti limp cold
casualty of their battle
warmth drained from the room

129

mozzarella gone
dreams melted like cheese never
gracing empty plates

130

they clean in silence
each pasta strand a sharp pain
each sauce stain a scar

131

kitchen battlefield
littered with remains of hope
bitterness lingers

132

thoughts of what could be
sweetness of mozzarella
ghost in empty hands

133

promises still loom
like shadows clinging to walls
haunting every step

134

they finish the task
kitchen spotless tension thick
air heavy with loss

135

broken love remains
etched in every empty plate
a night lost to words

136

dreams melt and slip through
like pasta through trembling hands
lost and never held

137

golden hair glistens
cascading like trapped sunlight
each strand a bright thread

138

sweat drips down her face
traces contours of effort
a glistening path

139

eyes hold a thousand
dreams and stories caught by one
simple and pure thing

140

a small puppy's gaze
eyes wide with untouched wonder
tail a blur of joy

141

furry burst of life
bounding into her bright world
bringing pure laughter

142

she bends down to reach
golden hair a light curtain
fingers tremble soft

143

the puppy licks slow
warm wet promise of friendship
a bond through chaos

144

she laughs clear and bright
like a bell cutting through weight
lightens her burden

145

golden hair a halo
sweat gleams like tiny jewels
proof of her journey

146

puppy by her feet
small eyes full of loyalty
anchor in the storm

147

amidst noise and sweat
she finds a new light within
a hope through struggle

148

she stands heart lighter
puppy at her side tail wagged
joy in small moments

149

steps sure and steady
golden hair catches the sun
heart open and full

150

each drop on her skin
a testament to her fight
to dreams she still holds

151

she knows in this breath
she is right where she should be
whole alive complete

152

there she remains still
in the middle of the flow
sage in liquid school

153

water rushes past
cold swift relentless force churns
but she stands firm strong

154

eyes sharp clear knowing
the madness of the world's spin
the folly of man

155

river flows onward
life's absurd and ever moving
a dance with no end

156

she shrugs grinning wide
embracing the wild chaos
her smile says it all

157

seen love and seen loss
beauty and horror's wild peaks
yet here she remains

158

feet planted on rock
feeling the push of currents
statue of spirit

159

life slips like water
moments flow through open hands
she savors each one

160

people pass and stare
some wave some shake heads and sigh
but she does not care

161

sun sets in gold light
she stands silhouette glowing
sage in a river

162

hair wild in the breeze
clothes soaked and clinging like skin
alive in the flow

163

laugh rings through the air
melody of joy defiance
yes life's a wild ride

164

river rushes on
she stays center unbroken
laughing at the tide

165

belching quarks explode
from distant neutron star cores
quasar flickers on

166

I sit on red shift
blowing kisses to nowhere
they loop back to me

167

galaxies expand
dots on an old balloon's curve
drifting through the void

168

exploding stars
ejaculate into night
fade to cold whispers

169

in cosmos's song
I am the faintest echo
lost in symphony

170

stars flare up then die
their brilliance a brief breath held
then gone to silence

171

quasar's ancient light
beams through darkened emptiness
lighthouse of lost time


172

I on this small rock
grain of sand in an abyss
cosmic shuffle's pawn


173

kisses cross the void
warmth of breath lost in vacuum
loop back through dark space


174

planets drift apart
on an endless stretching void
islands of nothing


175

exploding stars
their spent seed spreads through the dark
fades to quiet hums

176

I am but a speck
on a speck in endless night
fleeting thought of dust

177

nebulae swirl on
black holes feast in grand silence
universe turns still

178

belching out the quarks
dying stars build up new worlds
life born in endings

179

I send out my love
knowing it will never land
but send it anyway

180

even in death's grasp
creation still breathes something
beauty from chaos

181

galaxies drift wide
stars scream into silence
I remain watching

182

poet of the stars
lost in the inky vastness
searching for the threads

183

sitting on this rock
blowing kisses into night
waiting for return

184

until then I write
sending love into the void
a small distant light

185

part of this design
a tiny insignificant
pulse in endless waves

186

galaxies may drift
stars spreading out for ever
but I still reach out

187

aware alive here
a small part of something vast
knowing I belong

188

one damp tiny speck
holding meaning in the dark
making my own mark

189

kisses in the dark
tiny sparks of hope I send
into the still night

190

in life's endless dance
beauty and ugliness twine
each one shapes the other

191

world spins like a top
ballet of light and shadow
joy twirls with sorrow

192

one cannot exist
rose and thorn forever bound
each with the other

193

no dawn without night
grace paired with a hint of pain
woven in the weave

194

we walk the tightrope
balanced on the edge of both
pulled by life's fierce tide

195

in the quiet breath
beauty shines against despair
smiles through tears rise strong

196

they dance close as one
twin forces in lockstep spin
truth in every move

197

hold the darkness close
for it gives light its meaning
embrace the contrast

198

accept the raw dance
eternal waltz of what is
fragile fleeting truth

199

beauty blooms in pain
light shines brighter in the dark
it's all intertwined

200

potato flakes mixed
cement forms on my sad plate
meal gone wrong again

201

gray lump on the plate
a sad excuse for a meal
some things shouldn't be


202

kitchen lies silent
fridge hums softly in the dark
spoon heavy in hand


203

spoonful drips back down
thick unyielding like old dreams
solidifying


204

they said it was simple
just add water stir it well
but nothing is smooth


205

I take a slow bite
taste of disappointment thick
texture of regret

206

I swallow it down
because what else can you do
when food turns to stone


207

outside world spins on
people living striving strong
but here silence reigns


208

I push plate away
leave spoon resting where it fell
walk to window's light


209

world keeps on turning
even as chaos unfolds
in small rooms like mine


210

truth found in the clash
of opposites merging now
shaping all we are

211

this is all we have
this eternal give and take
the dance we call life


212

hardboiled egg sits still
badly peeled in kitchen sink
stinking and alone


213

shell cracked and broken
bits cling stubborn to the end
refusing to fall


214

it stinks of failure
simple tasks gone all awry
nothing fits quite right


215

just an egg they say
but it's more than just breakfast
a day slipping fast

216

tiny defeat grows
small weights piling up higher
too heavy to hold

217

tap water rushes
washing mess but not the scent
shell clings on stubborn

218

I laugh bitterly
egg a sad reminder here
of things falling through

219

a single egg sits
a quiet monument to
plans that fall apart

220

leave it in the sink
smell of failure lingers still
kitchen quiet dark

221

another fight lost
another day's small defeat
a badly peeled egg


222

pizza box in hand
walking out to morning's trash
thinking of last night


223

dawn light thin and pale
washes over empty streets
shuffle in slippers


224

box flops at my side
grease stains and crumbs tell the tale
another lost night


225

there were fireflies
soft flickers of gentle hope
in the darkened yard

226

beer in hand I watched
tiny mayflies in the night
fragile yet steady

227

reminding me then
that even in deepest dark
beauty still shines through

228

pizza long gone cold
laughter faded into dusk
just night and soft light

229

morning comes again
magic of mayflies fades
replaced by routine

230

trash can lid clanks shut
box discarded with the mess
memory remains

231

last night's mayflies dance
a whisper of what could be
in mundane moments

232

small stubborn flame glows
holds on in the gray of dawn
hinting at the more

233

I walk back inside
day stretches long before me
hold on to that light

234

fleeting fragile glimpse
of beauty in the shadows
a guide through the hours

235

struggle to exist
personalities like shade
shifting fluid forms

236

we wear masks and dance
play roles beneath bright stage lights
something raw clings close

237

mess of contradictions
beautifully flawed beings
seeking sense in flux

238

shadows stretch and shrink
but the core stays unbroken
heartbeat in the dark

239

we shift and we change
yet a light flickers within
through it all we laugh

240

faith's a strange old coat
found in the back of closets
just when needed most

241

worn coat around bones
keeps out the bitter cold's bite
comfort in darkness

242

I keep moving on
one step at a time through night
trusting the unseen

243

weight on weary back
won't break me no matter what
faith holds up my spine

244

I walk among ruins
where dreams fall like autumn leaves
wind whispers secrets

245

faces of the lost
broken weary hopeless eyes
searching for something

246

do they know the coat
grace wrapped tight against the storm
warm and sheltering

247

streetlights flicker faint
shadows dance on empty walls
men drown in cheap lies

248

in still night's silence
when the city breathes heavy
Divine grace lifts me

249

sit with them in silence
lift my glass in quiet prayer
witness to their pain

250

there's beauty in pain
moonlight on abandoned streets
dogs howl at the stars

251

solace found alone
knowing even in dark's grip
there's a light that shines

252

walking this set path
faith guiding each tired step
toward horizon's edge

253

the city's broken
people lost in empty streets
wandering for hope

254

but I walk with heart
believing cracks and shadows
hold a holy truth

255

and in dawn's first light
when day breaks the night's long hold
clarity returns

256

grace not just a word
but a promise that sustains
carries me onward

257

essence transforming
core nature shifting within
metamorphosis

258

profound changes stir
redefining spirit's depth
life reborn again

259

whiskey in the glass
last drag of a cigarette
dark alleys whisper

260

sleepless nights linger
where transformation takes hold
shadows shed their skins

261

we're all chrysalis
wrapped tight in our own dark lies
waiting for the break


262

that crack in the shell
when old skin falls to the ground
emerge raw and new


263

wings sting in the sun
tender to life's biting light
yet ready to fly


264

life a cruel sculptor
chipping at stone's rough edges
finding veins of gold


265

we shift and we grow
through the grime and the glitter
seeking what's hidden

266

stripping to essence
discovering what's beneath
truths that hold us close

267

when dust finally rests
when the last drink is poured out
we stand transformed whole

268

not perfect not pure
but real in spirit and soul
new life born from pain

269

she looks with disdain
scratches her arm like to say
you're just a mosquito

270

then comes the old dog
follows her like she's a queen
headed to her throne

271

I sit on the bench
slip off my worn-out oxford
stone falls to the ground

272

small chipped piece of rock
looks like it broke off a tomb
sharp with jagged edge

273

hard as old granite
stained with the blood of past steps
shoes worn past their prime

274

home where whiskey waits
typewriter mocks empty room
cat stares out at rain

275

pipe smoke curls and sways
wonder if it's all worth it
stumbling through each step

276

collecting life's stones
dreams tangled in my worn head
regrets in my heart

277

blonde's long gone by now
probably never saw me
or noticed the limp

278

dog off somewhere else
sniffing corners of this world
living in pure ease

279

back at my own desk
staring at blank screen's cold light
words refuse to come

280

stone in the fish tank
mocks me with its silent stare
like the world outside

281

living's a hot path
walking barefoot on sharp stones
not knowing the way

282

gravel in your shoes
sometimes you don't know it's there
but keep moving on

283

because what else is there
but to walk the crooked road
stone in shoe and all

284

dancing on the edge
igniting matches on fruit
fire meets decay's scent

285

howling at the moon
with nothing but a small comb
madness finds solace

286

labyrinthian halls
searching for the sun below
shadows breathe with light

287

barefoot on blood floors
eyes scorched by distant dunes' glare
steps echo despair

288

whirr of machines hum
symphony of cold breath sounds
grappling with no hands

289

pockets hold no truth
invisible mind breaks through
facade crumbles slow

290

clothed in old denials
clerical garb hides nothing
sadness stains the soul

291

amidst all decay
just a shadow of what was
adrift in chaos


292

hollow vessel floats
seeking grace in futile winds
echo in still halls


293

yet I move forward
corridors of uncertainty
grace flickers in dark


294

in autumn's garden
three old women sit in shade
hands like brittle twigs


295

silver hair like streams
one holds a mirror to dreams
time's whispers drift by

296

wrinkles speak of years
etched deep by yesterdays' sighs
door of echoes closed

297

eyes that once shone bright
another clutches her book
pages thick with life

298

pen flows through the past
joy and sorrow intertwine
fearing words unsaid

299

no fear of the edge
only the past's quiet steps
fading into dust

300

under oak's broad arms
laughter mingles with their tears
sacred space of peace

301

night falls with calm grace
stars light up their final sighs
cosmic fears erased

302

whispering winds speak
depths of sea murmur softly
rocks hold sacred truths

303

hidden holy space
sanctuary of the soul
yearning's quiet breath

304

bird songs fill the air
longing for a home unknown
grief for lost landscapes

305

nostalgia's deep ache
for places we've never been
paths we cannot tread

306

scent of pine and light
sun's warmth on an aching heart
birdsong's tender note


307

traces linger here
of nowhere and everywhere
Divine presence felt


308

light beyond the dark
guiding through storm and shadow
hope's flame flickers strong


309

connection remains
to what is greater than us
silent thread of grace


310

dawn's stillness whispers
chaos storms with holy touch
sunset's kiss holds peace

311

glimpses of Divine
echoes of soul's timeless quest
sacredness revealed

312

three coins slip from grasp
soft chimes on cold concrete floor
echoes of stillness

313

time halts in descent
silver circles in faint light
mundane turns sacred

314

each coin a symbol
of giving receiving flow
all things intertwined

315

resting where they fell
glittering in the silence
a prayer in light

316

gratitude blooms here
simple beauty in three coins
singing their own song

317

life's cacophony
arrives like scattered raindrops
each note solitary

318

grasping at moments
puzzle pieces of our days
fragments of a whole

319

broken shards reveal
reflections of our own selves
mirrors cracked but clear

320

people scattered too
each part of the greater whole
seeking unity

321

amidst brokenness
a glimmer of hope still shines
smile through the darkness

322

calling for wholeness
Divine glue to bind our souls
mend what's torn apart

323

bodies minds and hearts
woven in deep connection
tapestry of light

324

gazing in her eyes
not just a person we see
but Divine essence

325

in still workshop's calm
stonemason's daughter cradles
world's child in her arms

326

her eyes deep as night
reflecting infinite stretch
hope in empty space

327

child's grasp meets the void
nourishment cannot be found
tears of frozen grief

328

kisses the child's brow
caught in love and resentment
held by both at once

329

workshop's form fades out
leaving only her and pain
taste of ash lingers

330

yet hope flickers faint
fragile thread of existence
human spirit holds

331

dance of existence
ebb and flow of earthly life
balance found within

332

restless soul seeks growth
yet too much or too little
throws it off the path

333

burdened poor seek food
drenched by rain clouds of despair
survival's harsh call

334

wealthy grasp at gain
shielded by abundance's veil
anchored in reward

335

two hearts intertwined
held by threads of sweet and sharp
never torn apart

336

who am I who seeks
echoes deep in soul's chambers
where truth and peace meet

337

essence of true Zen
inquiry without end lies
path of pure stillness

338

balance the middle
embracing life's mystery
content in the now

339

in the vast stillness
where time and space softly blend
something stirs beyond

340

no bounds no limits
unconditional presence
wraps the whole of life

341

nothing can escape
no part of self left untouched
by its gentle reach

342

it stretches so far
beyond what mind can fathom
infinite embrace

343

to touch such a force
is to meet the Divine's face
silent and immense

344

truth walks a pathless
road unfolding before us
beyond belief's gate

345

not chained by dogma
nor by the walls of sects closed
truth flows ever free

346

to seek truth alone
a journey through empty lands
guided from within

347

no maps no markers
just whispers in soul's dark night
glimmer in shadow

348

truth's many mansions
stand with doors of faith and love
each open to light

349

some walk by reason
others by the heart's soft steps
all paths weave as one

350

each door leads onward
to God's vast and open arms
welcoming all souls

351

in the meek calm heart
where gentleness conquers all
softness breaks stone walls

352

like breeze through green leaves
or stream carving stubborn rock
gentle shifts the world

353

God dwells in stillness
in space without shape or form
touching the unseen

354

power lies not strong
but in surrender's deep flow
we become pure light

355

in the wise soul's core
clarity dwells quietly
anchored deep in peace

356

not from worldly thoughts
but through knowing the Divine
wisdom flows like spring

357

centered within God
beyond life's restless turning
she stands calm and clear

358

for she sees the truth
richness beyond what eyes see
all flows from within

359

though her form may fade
spirit remains ever tied
to the endless source

360

what does a man know
at the end of the long road
but the breath of night

361

death stirs old fears deep
calls softly from the shadows
whispers of return

362

forgive me I plead
if I don't know or don't care
life's cruel joke unfolds

363

a parade of fools
chasing ghosts in empty fields
dreams falling like leaves

364

sand slips through my hands
each grain a moment gone past
each hope a lost cause

365

take my hand my friend
walk me to where the path ends
where light meets the dark

366

we'll stand on the edge
watch the sun sink low and fade
let sorrows drift off

367

truth just a word carved
from the wood of fragile hearts
splintered by the weight

368

promises shatter
fears rise up and overwhelm
trust crumbles to dust

369

what does a man know
but the vastness of death's grip
the endless night's call

370

yet in that dark void
bright moments linger like stars
laughter shared love lost

371

tiny joys remain
the light of a fleeting glance
a smile in the rain

372

forgive me I'm lost
if I seem a little mad
life's a lovely mess

373

a puzzle undone
a story with no clear end
just the muddled middle

374

where we stumble on
fall rise and try once again
bruised hearts still beating

375

take my hand lead me
to where the last breath drifts off
let me face it all

376

unflinching unbowed
eyes wide open to the void
I've seen the dance fade


377

shadow mingles light
birth turns into death then back
cycles never cease


378

what do I know now
only that I'm here with you
and that's all we need


379

no answers just trust
fragile threads that hold us close
even as we break


380

take my hand let's go
wander into the unknown
meet it without fear

381

we're just travelers
searching for meaning for grace
lost in this big world

382

if we find it or not
it doesn't matter at all
the journey's enough

383

each step that we take
each moment shared held in breath
that's everything

384

take my hand my friend
walk with me into the night
that's all that we need

385

the journey's the path
the road that we walk with hope
that's our truth our light

386

evening stretches long
stars and galaxies lift off
into endless night

387

whispers of the sky
cascade of cosmic dust falls
velvet dark and deep

388

maidens of delight
please rescue me from this veil
of unending tears

389

lost in the chaos
drowning in vastness of space
the night's silent scream

390

eyes stare back at me
no form just the eyes remain
taste the unknown world

391

juice of distant lands
flows from here to the far edge
where dreams drift away

392

finished is the word
to consume all other words
but summer's touch waits

393

come to me in spring
bright blooms soft whispering winds
give these flowers to God

394

a frail man limps on
his heart a fragile puzzle
broken yet still whole

395

justice by his side
a shadowed figure shrouded
walking edge of night

396

steps echo through dark
pain etched deep within each step
each breath survival

397

stars scatter above
distant beacons in the sky
is there more than this

398

maidens far away
their laughter a faint echo
dreams gone with the breeze

399

wandering alone
a solitary figure
lost in vast expanse

400

yet his eyes still shine
a spark of defiant hope
refusing to break

401

he tastes the unknown
sips from life's uncertainty
finds solace in change

402

flowers offered up
to the Divine's open hands
beauty in broken

403

give these blooms to God
a release a soft surrender
to something greater

404

all frail men we are
broken hearts and weary feet
seeking that same light

405

stars and galaxies
lift from earth's grasp drifting on
sea of entropy

406

standing on the edge
gazing deep into the void
he still finds peace

407

accepts what he sees
vast universe unknowable
simply being here

408

migraine comes and goes
like snows tapping on glass panes
silent rhythmic thrum

409

a ghostly presence
whispering in my ears soft
borrowing my time

410

it shows me stained glass
hidden relics in crypts deep
beauty edged with pain

411

on mountain tops high
or at the deepest sea trench
its shimmer lingers

412

when I sip my tea
or crack an egg in silence
it haunts my quiet

413

a parasite light
glowing growing shrinking fast
in shadows it fades

414

driving with me close
a passenger in the dark
fracturing my sight

415

my eyes wrestle on
caught between pain and stillness
bound till freed again

416

in my suffering
broken pieces of the world
reflect soft colors

417

each shard a window
to realms where pain and beauty
dance as one and same

418

relics in my soul
whisper of saints and battles
etched in dark silence

419

stained glass thoughts shimmer
in hues of anguish and awe
a fragile beauty

420

guiding through the fog
my migraine a beacon strong
blurring light and dark

421

a witness to all
it sits beside me at work
watching over me

422

never truly gone
it glows then fades a shadow
always at the edge

423

eyes more than windows
they glimpse beyond the surface
to where pain resides

424

a waltz of light dark
dancing agony beauty
in my broken gaze

425

I accept its weight
the delicate fragile dance
the sorrow and grace

426

my eyes burn with tears
seeing the fallen blossoms
caught in the spring breeze

427

the wind gently plays
with petals of a lost hope
whispering farewell

428

a sparrow flutters
settles on the empty branch
chirps a song of loss

429

old pond empty now
once filled with koi and laughter
ripples with silence

430

even the pine tree
bows its head to the quiet
as dusk softly fades

431

tea cools in the cup
left untouched on the table
steam mingles with sighs

432

the scent of pine smoke
drifts through the small open door
like a lingering dream

433

fireflies return home
to fields where no one watches
yet they keep glowing

434

the moon pale and full
casts long shadows on the ground
highlighting my grief

435

in the hush of night
the cicadas sing alone
calling out for peace

436

how fragile we are
like dew drops on morning leaves
vanishing at dawn

437

the old willow weeps
for those who have gone away
never to return

438

beneath the plum tree
I lay down my weary heart
and rest in silence

439

soft rain gently falls
washing away yesterday
leaving only now

440

pain makes me better
tears fall like spring rain on blooms
each drop feeds the roots

441

flowers grow brighter
from the sorrow in my chest
soft petals of light

442

pain flows like rivers
through the garden of my soul
quenching silent thirst

443

each tear tells a tale
of nights spent alone with grief
turning dark to dawn

444

what blossoms from pain
holds the sunlight in its veins
glowing through the storm

445

even in shadows
petals find a way to bloom
in tears they take flight

446

suffering whispers
secrets to the waiting earth
each sob plants a seed

447

pain is the gardener
tending to the fields of loss
cultivating hope

448

every tear that falls
waters dreams that might have wilted
into something new

449

flowers thank my pain
for the light it brings to them
and for the chance to grow

450

a child brings her doll
to be blessed by sacred hands
small faith in small arms

451

who is this child now
wrapped in wisdom's purple glow
Sofia crowned bright

452

her doll soft and worn
becomes echoes of my past
innocence long lost

453

we walk to the stream
to bathe in light and shadow
river's cool embrace

454

each drop a whisper
of the Son's love and the Father's
flowing through my doubts

455

forgive me silence
when my lips cannot shape words
swallowed by the void

456

my blurred eyes can't see
the endless dance of the stars
or beauty's soft hymn

457

forgive deaf ears closed
to dawn's first cracking of shells
new life stirring deep

458

but I stand and drink
from salvation's endless flow
each sip a small prayer

459

Sofia's sweet voice
drifts through wind carries secrets
lost in time's vast breeze

460

she knows what we've lost
songs buried under the noise
hymns of earth and sky

461

in her eyes worlds bloom
woven from light and sorrow
truths we've all let fade

462

hand in hand we walk
to the river of mercy
red roses pressed to her chest

463

the water stings cold
but clears away doubt's thick dust
purifying fears

464

we taste holy flesh
a communion of spirit
bonds that never break

465

we're held in His love
a warmth that fills every crack
healing hollow hearts

466

if I stumble here
and my hands shake from the weight
forgive me I'm small

467

forgive the child's voice
trembling reaching for hope's hand
learning how to sing

468

beneath the waterfall
I'll stand washed in endless grace
finding strength to see

469

Sofia's whisper
and the doll's quiet blessing
carry me through night

470

the sacred hymn calls
joining stars rivers and wind
in a song of love

471

and I too will sing
with faltering voice made strong
in the hymn of grace

472

trauma lingers on
like grease at the pan's bottom
stubborn unmoving

473

seeps deep in the soul
turns bright days into shadows
taints joy with sorrow

474

broken sleep at night
echoes of wounds long since made
ringing like old bells

475

a cruel lullaby
sung in whispers only you
hear in silent hours

476

dust in your inner ear
tiny specks of lost moments
cling like second skin

477

you try to scrub clean
the stains that refuse to leave
etched deep in your bones

478

laughter mixed with grief
smiles shadowed by memories
weighing down each breath

479

searching for solace
you find fleeting peace at best
like light through thick fog

480

yet still you believe
in hope that refuses death
even in darkness

481

beyond dreams beyond
the dust and lingering fear
a spark still remains

482

night demons arise
you face them with desperate strength
fight to reclaim self

483

a warrior's heart
knows scars are badges of pain
yet they show courage

484

though dirt may remain
you learn to see it with grace
not every stain leaves

485

you are more than pain
more than the ghosts of what's lost
you rise from ruins

486

step by step you walk
breath by breath you find your way
through sorrow's harsh storm

487

trauma makes you sick
but in it there's testament
to all you've endured

488

beyond dreams beyond
dust and shadows of despair
you keep moving on

489

finding strength in scars
finding light in fractured cracks
beauty in broken

490

you carry it all
with grace transforming the weight
into your own strength

491

through the darkest nights
you choose to keep on living
to rise fight and heal

492

you are more than pain
you are survival pure light
shining through the dark

493

she is wabi-sabi
a quiet beauty unfolds
in her small details

494

incomplete she stands
a work in progress by time
etched with life's patina

495

her flaws are her charm
the essence of her being
a gentle presence

496

modest and humble
grace found in simple moments
elegance of breath

497

she treads on the earth
with a lightness all her own
each step a whisper

498

between air and ground
a specter of subtlety
soft in her silence

499

her shoes worn and loved
ribbons of stories untold
each piece a journey

500

on the crowded train
she is small between the seats
a faint murmur felt

501

seen by open hearts
lost in the noise of the world
she bridges the gaps

502

with kittens and wine
she soothes the aching spirits
laughter in the storm

503

vague and undefined
she drifts in and out of view
fog in morning light

504

a living poem
soft curves of butternut squash
pastel hues of dawn

505

stripped to the essence
yet leaves room for mystery
lingering wonder

506

her presence a glimpse
of something fleeting yet real
caught in the corner

507

true beauty exists
not in flawless symmetry
but in worn edges

508

simply she is art
painted by the hands of fate
each line tells a tale

509

in her you can see
the world as it truly is
broken yet perfect

510

worn with time's embrace
she is a mosaic bright
shining through her cracks

511

sit with them in silence
lift my glass in quiet prayer
witness to their pain


512

not as it should be
but as it is in pure form
beauty in the raw


513

each imperfection
a note in nature's songbook
a melody soft


514

the power of time
weaving scars into her skin
grace in the weathered


515

poetry of life
in her unpolished smile
the world finds its voice

516

the earth whispers low
echoes of my quiet soul
rustling through the leaves

517

in the river's flow
I hear the song of my heart
woven in currents

518

each breath of the breeze
the warmth of sun on my skin
reflects who I am

519

tied to land and sky
in the dance of shifting tides
I find my solace

520

how seasons move on
a rhythm deep in my bones
calling me to peace

521

all nature's voices
sing a song of unity
harmony and grace

522

Jesus speaks of love
through his hands we glimpse Divine
God's light made human

523

words of grace and truth
illuminate each shadow
mercy breathes in us

524

he bridges heaven
touches earth with gentleness
guiding us through light

525

God eternal being
beyond time beyond our grasp
holds us in stillness

526

no dualities
only boundless pure presence
a truth beyond self

527

the wise one walks free
her light brightens each shadow
a guide through the void

528

emptiness fulfilled
she flows with the universe
grace poured through silence

529

in her gentle calm
a beacon of endless love
unbound by the self

530

when breath fades away
in the hush of what's to come
truth wakes like dawn light

531

life a holy thread
each choice a woven pattern
on the cloth of time

532

every word we speak
ripples through the vast unknown
echoing in hearts

533

in reflection's calm
we see how each act connects
all beings as one

534

each deed carries weight
each thought shapes the endless path
touching distant lives

535

in silence we know
our lives are reflections cast
on existence's stream

536

the fairness of life
fits in a small thimble's depth
a drop of water

537

wait for the floodgates
forty days and forty nights
then loose the demons

538

each one with a chain
tied around its stubborn neck
cast into the sea

539

if the sea turns red
the sun will rise next morning
sand replaces blood

540

go to the shoreline
repeat this ritual prayer
until truth appears

541

fairness is a myth
we tell ourselves in the dark
to keep fear at bay


542

demons drown and rise
wearing new collars new eyes
same old haunted gaze


543

the sea now a desert
red waves turned to shifting dunes
dreams lost in the wind


544

each grain of pale sand
holds a memory's soft weight
whispers of what's gone


545

we walk on the shore
collecting fragile fragments
of what could have been

546

the fairness we seek
a mirage on the skyline
always out of reach

547

close your eyes for years
let silence fill the long night
truth will gently speak

548

life a cruel jest
a punchline in the cosmos
unheard yet felt deep

549

fairness a shadow
a dance of light and darkness
fleeting fragile glimpse

550

open your eyes wide
see the small black spot of truth
staining your heart's core

551

life is what it is
raw and wild joy and sorrow
woven threads unseen

552

tell me what you know
about fairness in the dark
and I'll speak of tears

553

of laughter's echo
of the touch of a lover
the pain of goodbye

554

the warmth of sunrise
the chill of a moonless night
all things bound in one

555

place it in a cup
wait forty days nights of rain
open floodgates wide

556

let the shadows out
watch them swirl and dance again
across the vast sea

557

we all share these chains
searching for a kind of peace
bound by unseen threads

558

walk the endless beach
collect grains of sand and hope
fairness in silence

559

hold to what you can
truth slips through like grains of sand
falling to the sea

560

tell me what is fair
what lies beyond joy and pain
in life's rough pattern

561

we all seek meaning
hoping to catch something pure
in chaos and loss


562

a Sunday somewhere
eggplant and cabbage simmer
bean curd with a pinch


563

clams dance on the plate
a baby's foot on grandma's knee
bounces to laughter


564

the scent of fried fish
drifts with a kitten's soft meow
walls hold handprints close


565

a dog wags his tail
window open to the breeze
sunflowers in flight

566

mushrooms roll along
playing tag with peas that came
all the way from Brooklyn

567

they pose for a pic
peas too caught in the moment
smiles locked in the lens

568

then outside to play
sunlight stretches long shadows
laughter fills the air

569

baby's giggle bright
grandma's smile a soft crescent
dog chasing the ball

570

kitten on the sill
watching with wide eyed wonder
joy echoes around

571

it's a Sunday's peace
amid the world's wild turmoil
a calm in the storm

572

the sky blushing pink
as the sun sets in the west
day's warmth still lingers

573

eggplant and cabbage
bean curd and salt on the tongue
simple tastes that fill

574

the soul more deeply
than any grand feast might reach
soft comforts remain

575

gathered together
one last time before night falls
loved ones side by side

576

bound by shared moments
weaving stories through the day
life's simple magic

577

stars begin to twirl
the world quiets day slips past
memories soft glow

578

and somewhere we find
beauty in the simplest things
love in just being

579

the one who grieves walks
bucket of unshed tears heavy
weighed down by sorrow

580

each step on the sand
a soft mark of silent pain
etched by loss and time

581

he reaches the shore
where the sea meets his burden
waves wait unconcerned

582

with trembling hands he pours
each tear into the ocean
lost in its vastness

583

the waves swallow whole
what took years to accumulate
a drop in the sea

584

the ocean does not care
never has never will
just takes and moves on

585

his bucket now bare
yet his heart remains so full
of echoes of love

586

of moments long gone
now shadows in the mind's halls
ghosts that will not fade


587

he watches the sea
where sky kisses horizon
wonders if pain ebbs


588

if tides of sorrow
will one day leave him washed clean
made whole once again


589

the waves hum softly
a lullaby of longing
a song of farewell


590

for a moment peace
in the rhythm of the waves
in grief's gentle pull

591

others walked this path
poured their sadness to the sea
and found solace there

592

he just stands and waits
bucket empty heart still full
wind carries prayers

593

to the distant waves
hopes the tides will one day turn
sorrow left behind

594

but for now he stays
grief's weight still in his weary bones
lost in the ocean

595

and the waves roll on
relentless uncaring sea
bearing silent grief

596

and somewhere we find
beauty in the simplest things
love in just being

597

I rush to his side
heat searing through my worn shoes
arms open heart raw

598

is there something please
I can do anything friend
to ease your torment

599

kill me he cries out
voice a desperate plea raw
reaching to the sky

600

fingers point to God
who dwells in stone sanctuaries
deaf to cries of pain

601

eyes wild with despair
search for mercy for a sign
find only the sun

602

blazing without care
a relentless glaring force
mocking his anguish

603

I kneel close to him
heart heavy with helplessness
feeling all his fear

604

kill me kill me please
a broken prayer whispered low
lost in the cruel wind

605

I want to tell him
that he's not at fault no sin
brought him to this place

606

we're all victims here
trapped in life's unyielding snare
under hearts who sleep


607

but words are hollow
a poor balm for a deep wound
no comfort no peace


608

so I hold his hand
share the silence of his pain
a witness to grief


609

pavement scorches on
sun blazes in the high noon
time stretches a void


610

kill me he whispers
his voice now just a faint breeze
truth heavy as stone

611

I want to save him
to take this burden from him
but I am just flesh

612

tied to my own chains
unable to change his fate
bound by my limits

613

still I stay with him
offering what little grace
a hand a heartbeat

614

a man writhes in pain
on the scorching black asphalt
and I sit with him

615

I pray silently
to a God who hasn't left
a God who still sees

616

not distant in stone
but here in the heat the dust
sharing in the pain

617

and I see my God
writhing on this pavement too
bearing all our grief

618

this broken stranger
suffering beneath the sun
is not alone now

619

for in his torment
God's presence is here with him
not in some cold hall

620

lying on the ground
feeling every searing burn
sharing every wound

621

a man writhes in pain
and God is beside him too
kneeling on the stones


622

man in the mirror
grapples with his restless past
ghosts whisper softly


623

memories surface
from the shadows of long nights
sting of bitter truth


624

he recalls her laugh
woman in the red dress gone
rain hides her footsteps


625

goodbye on her lips
her voice fades like mist in rain
echoes through his mind

626

lights another smoke
years blur into wisps of pain
constant unwelcome

627

whiskey numbs his soul
arms of strangers soothe the ache
but grief always wins

628

father's calloused hands
belt and bottle taught him pain
love left in bruises

629

scars line flesh and bone
testament of fear and rage
childhood shadows cling

630

empty barroom hush
bartender sees but won't speak
silence drowns sorrow

631

one more shot it burns
keeps memories at the edge
but can't erase them


632

cheap motel stained sheets
women come and go like dreams
cold dawns always wake


633

friends lost on hard streets
graveside tears why them not me
weight of life's cruel jest


634

mirror's aged reflection
each wrinkle a story told
etched by time and loss


635

not young not unscathed
but he's still here still holding
hope's thin thread remains

636

lifts his glass in toast
to battles fought scars embraced
to the ghosts that haunt

637

tonight he'll face them
one by one in barroom light
seek peace in the pain

638

jukebox plays a tune
melancholy notes of hope
melody softens

639

breathes deep smoke and grief
exhales with a hint of calm
resolve flickers bright

640

ghosts will always lurk
memories won't fade away
but he's still alive

641

glass raised to himself
to the man still standing strong
fighting through the night

642

new day will arrive
dawn breaks with the light of hope
promise of new paths

643

somewhere something more
waits beyond the restless dark
better days ahead

644

he'll hold on to that
as the hours stretch and fade
holding firm to hope

645

man in the mirror
faces shadows of the past
yet still he stands tall

646

and for that he drinks
a toast to survival's grace
to life's small victories

647

together we walked
into the mist of shadows
searching for answers

648

the air thick with dreams
whispers of forgotten worlds
pressed against our hearts

649

a horizon blurred
neither day nor night we sought
the truth in twilight

650

hand in hand we moved
each step echoing our fears
each breath a question

651

I confessed to her
that I knew nothing of it
the world beyond death

652

scripture's words a map
but the path was faint and lost
in the fog of time

653

the city of light
rose before us in the dark
spires touching stars

654

we approached slowly
eyes wide with both hope and fear
ghosts watched from the gates

655

we entered its streets
time bending like a river
carrying us on

656

faces without names
souls who had forgotten love
yearning for something

657

in a quiet nook
we found the library's glow
pages filled with light

658

parables of faith
promises of grace and peace
danced just out of reach

659

the words of Jesus
beautiful yet elusive
lingered like soft smoke

660

meanings slipping by
like shadows in moonlit fields
offering no truth

661

the walls began to fade
as we were carried along
to a place of spring

662

flowers bloomed in hues
no earthly eye had yet seen
songs filled the warm air

663

she turned and asked me
is this heaven that we sought
is this the afterlife

664

I held her hand close
said I did not truly know
perhaps just a dream

665

in a garden's peace
we lay beneath silver leaves
souls warmed by their glow

666

in that fleeting time
our questions ceased to matter
love was all we knew

667

the music of hope
softly washed over our fears
golden light embraced

668

maybe this is it
not a place of clear answers
but a dream of love

669

a realm without end
where love finds rest in the shade
of life's mystery

670

where each step we take
becomes the journey itself
each breath a promise

671

so we close our eyes
held by the boundless unknown
content to just be

672

no answers needed
for love is the light that stays
even when we leave

673

maybe that's the truth
not a heaven or a hell
but love's quiet grace

674

a place where we rest
souls intertwined with wonder
in the endless dusk

675

Silent chapel breath
whispered prayers rise like smoke
God's voice in the wind

676

essence unfolding
nature shifts within us all
metamorphosis


677

sacred moment here
rooted in earth's embrace deep
miracles breathe life


678

journeying inward
waking to wonder's bright gaze
healing begins now


679

life's shadow struggle
personalities flicker
truth remains steadfast


680

remove the veils Lord
let inner light shine brightly
truth of who we are

681

each pure exchange shared
reflects the Divine within
we touch and we grow

682

grant me courage now
to show myself as I am
vulnerable true

683

life's winding journey
remember divinity
linked to creation

684

when your voice fades Lord
and silence fills the wide gap
we build false idols

685

forgive me O Lord
for relying on the lies
crafted from my fear

686

straying from your light
peace becomes a distant dream
cold hearts divided

687

in your mercy Lord
guide our broken steps back home
let love make us whole

688

amid life's sharp strain
patient hope a steadfast friend
calm descends softly

689

life's burdens still weigh
but knowing you're here with me
brings courage brings peace

690

labels cannot bind
the spirit's boundless journey
truth transcends all bounds

691

in deep existence
our soul's ultimate concern
reaches beyond traits


692

when despair clouds hope
fragile beauty still persists
like flowers in frost


693

from deep desolation
a hand rises up gently
hope reborn through touch


694

tangled dance of life
beauty holds ugliness close
each one intertwined


695

circus of moments
we spin dance then fade away
time's fleeting ballet

696

guide us to still peace
from chaos bring us comfort
harmony restored

697

with each breath release
grant me peace in present time
tethered to your love

698

peace fills this green earth
miracles in being here
present I find peace

699

the wind's soft whispers
echo through the stillness here
grief in every breeze

700

in life's fleeting hours
we find small fragile moments
where beauty endures

701

yearning calls me home
nostalgia's soft ache within
for places long lost

702

pine's scent fills the air
sun's warmth settles on my skin
birds sing ancient songs

703

even in chaos
hope rises like morning sun
light in darkest nights

704

three old women sit
underneath autumn's old oak
hands like worn branches

705

time has left its mark
etched deep within every crease
wrinkles tell their tales

706

she fears closing doors
echoes of unspoken dreams
words left in journals

707

under stars' bright gaze
where shadows and light converge
peace rests in twilight

708

on sanity's edge
dancing with absurdity
finding solace there

709

seeking unseen light
barefoot through the darkened halls
truth hides in silence

710

gentle words touch deep
nectar sweet upon my tongue
fills each empty space

711

with love's embrace near
fear and pain slowly dissolve
trust in what will be


712

in dawn's quiet breath
the heart's burdens lift and fade
peace flows through silence


713

stillness fills the soul
Divine essence intertwined
with life's pulse complete


714

innocent children
orphaned by war's cold embrace
cry to stars above


715

love their only plea
gentle touch to heal their wounds
grant them hope's bright light

716

in a shattered world
let compassion be our guide
sorrow's bonds released


717

liberate us all
from the chains of hate and fear
in your light we rise


718

in your love we trust
fortified by strength within
to embrace the world


719

essence pure and bright
life's truth flows beyond all bounds
embracing the whole


720

in self's yielding space
we surrender to your light
walking paths unknown

721

hands that lift and hold
hearts that open wide to love
grace in every touch


722

each step leads us home
to love's infinite embrace
in silence we yield


723

there in stillness deep
questions fade into soft peace
and I say yes Lord


724

yes to what may come
to the unknown yet unseen
faith guides every breath


725

since that fleeting time
I've learned the art of release
not looking behind

726

embracing the now
faith and mystery in dance
presence fills my soul

727

on self's humble path
trusting the Divine design
led by unseen hands

728

struggling with dark
amidst shadows and sorrow
death lingered so near

729

yet hope's whisper broke
through the heavy weight of loss
piercing through despair

730

a light flickered near
soft promise in endless night
guiding with its glow

731

in webs we weave tight
fear binds hearts souls disconnected
yearning to break free

732

silent in between
walls of distrust crumble down
empathy builds bridges

733

souls embrace the calm
barriers dissolve like mist
love's connection forms

734

in that quiet space
unity begins to bloom
peace found in shared light

735

the Divine's vast breath
gives life to both shade and light
cosmos in each pulse

736

essence in silence
in whispers of time and space
God beyond our grasp

737

in your presence grace
infinite unseen yet felt
all creation sings

738

spirits freed from chains
of illusion's grasping hold
truth found in release

739

hearts soar wings outstretched
free from fear in love's pure light
peace within unfolds

740

each soul a beacon
in the still night shining bright
guiding hearts to truth

741

when destined souls meet
their lights intertwine and blend
seamless in their glow

742

union born of love
illuminates the darkness
together they shine

743

in the quiet room
shadows speak of what once was
stories left unsaid

744

old woman on rock
staring at the river's flow
wrinkles hold her grief

745

silver hair in wind
memories in every crease
heart heavy with loss

746

soul adrift searching
for peace on this river's shore
seeking solace near

747

in the belly's depth
Jonah wrestles with his past
finds his own shadow

748

shadows meet the light
boundless kinship in the dark
grace in solitude

749

from darkness to peace
freedom found in still embrace
whale's breath life renewed

750

in the stillness deep
even in belly's embrace
whispers speak of hope

751

service wearies hearts
not sin's burden but love's weight
grace calls for stillness

752

pause rest in silence
the river's ebb and surge flows
soul's renewal blooms

753

rest finds sanctuary
in garden's quiet embrace
grace flows from within

754

not in ceaseless toil
but in still moments of peace
spirit finds new life

755

Sisyphus stands still
stone rests beside tired feet
birds mock from above

756

detached he observes
endless sky of weary grief
pain's burdenless void

757

within his own song
echoes of grace and belonging
lost in search now found

758

sit with them in silence
lift my glass in quiet prayer
witness to their pain

759

kissing the child's brow
softness meets a distant storm
quiet love and grief

760

joy is a clear stream
resentment a restless wave
flowing side by side

761

hands cradle gently
yet the weight of sacrifice
presses in the space

762

we find in small acts
a way to keep holding on
through shadows of pain

763

knock on doors call out
through darkness I am still here
waiting by your side

764

each soft touch each step
a testament to our bond
even through the dark

765

together we face
the loneliness and despair
until light returns

766

since that fleeting time
I've learned the art of release
not looking behind

767

embracing the now
faith and mystery in dance
each breath a small grace

768

on self's winding path
trusting the unseen design
led by love's soft hand

769

struggling through dark
facing shadows of sorrow
death lingered so near

770

hope's whisper broke through
piercing the heavy silence
a soft tender yes

771

in the deepest night
a light flickered faint yet bright
hope's glow in the void

772

even in despair
truth and purpose still remain
guiding through the dark

773

webs of fear we weave
hearts bound tight distrust divides
yet hope bridges gaps

774

quiet in between
walls of distrust crumble down
empathy takes root

775

souls meet and embrace
barriers dissolve like mist
light found in shared breath

776

in that silent space
unity begins to bloom
hearts connect as one

777

Divine's breath expands
giving life to light and shade
each pulse a soft hymn

778

essence in stillness
unseen there yet deeply felt
God beyond all grasp

779

your presence pure grace
infinite yet here and now
all creation sings

780

boundless solitude
deep freedom in surrender
truth found in release

781

from soul's deepest depths
light emerges bright and clear
heaven's beacon near

782

two destined souls meet
their lights blend and intertwine
radiant love grows

783

when hearts softly touch
union born of love and trust
brilliance fills the night

784

in a quiet room
shadows whisper memories
dreams float in still air

785

old woman on rock
staring at the river's flow
wrinkles hold her grief

786

silver hair in wind
each crease tells a thousand tales
life's sorrow etched deep

787

soul adrift searching
for peace on the river's edge
solace near yet far

788

Jonah in the dark
finds kinship within the beast
grace in belly's hold

789

shadows meet the light
hope and fear in deep embrace
self's truth softly found

790

service wearies hearts
even love's gentle burden
calls for quiet rest

791

rest in stillness deep
let spirit's whispers be heard
peace blooms in silence

792

not in endless toil
but in moments of stillness
life's meaning revealed

793

Sisyphus breathes deep
stone rests at his weary feet
time's pulse slow and calm

794

detached he gazes
endless sky of grief and hope
pain's burden grows light

795

in his song's soft notes
echoes of grace and longing
solace found in pain

796

tenement shadows
soul drifts in a fog of days
one eared cat nearby

797

through thick glasses dim
each step a search for meaning
solace found in care

798

silent knocks echo
through rooms filled with quiet grief
my hand waits for you

799

we find in small acts
a way to keep holding on
through sorrow's shadow

800

each soft touch each step
a testament to our bond
light shared through the night

801

together we face
the loneliness and despair
until dawn returns

802

even those who stray
possibility remains
grace does not give up

803

blind cat seems to stare
in the distance searching still
for birds lost to sight

804

reading my poems
to you in the quiet dusk
perhaps you'll drift off

805

the cat softly purrs
moon rises through drifting clouds
ecstasy arrives

806

are we in decline
rabbi shrugs the silence speaks
answers lost in dust

807

monk slides on thin ice
cat's grin fish caught in sharp teeth
winter's playful jest

808

robes like broken wings
flutter on slippery ground
faith tested by ice

809

silent prayer falls
slipping into the night's void
cold bites at belief

810

cat in moon's shadow
silver scales gleam in soft light
mischief in its eyes

811

winter breathes harsh gusts
tearing through the monk's resolve
warmth is but a ghost

812

a stumble a fall
faith teeters on frozen ground
prayers lost in the wind

813

ice cracks beneath feet
hope shatters like brittle glass
emptiness echoes

814

life's cruel jest plays on
monk slides cat laughs in the dark
fish swims in dreams still

815

each step on thin ice
monk cat fish in cosmic dance
winter holds them close

816

city lights far off
mocking with their empty glow
shadows chase shadows

817

slip slide fate's cruel game
monk prays cat prowls fish vanishes
winter's grip holds tight

818

in the morning light
the monk still walks cat still hunts
winter laughs again

819

fleeting faith quick dreams
prayers melt on indifferent ice
laughter fades to cold

820

fried fish scent wafts high
stinking clam and spilled milk's scent
dog laps up sorrow

821

kitchen's chaos reigns
grease flies like a battlefield
clam reeks of lost dreams


822

milk pools on the floor
a river of regret flows
dog drinks unaware


823

by the table's edge
beer in hand cigarette low
watching mess unfold


824

fried fish smells linger
echoes of dinners long gone
laughter now a ghost


825

clam's stench rises strong
failure wrapped in brine's sour grasp
milk innocence lost

826

dog's world simple pure
licking up each drop of life
no fear of what's next

827

in smoke's curling rise
roads not taken haunt the room
choices left behind

828

fried fish in the air
a dog's tongue erases hope
future swirls in scent

829

dog wags tail in glee
mess and peace in chaos blend
find joy in the wreck

830

in a quiet room
tiny fly rests on the floor
unseen by searching cat

831

on soft bread mattress
an unseen guest finds refuge
cockroach feels at home

832

humble beauty breathes
life's harmony found in stillness
in simplest moments

833

paths to spirit's light
meander through winding ways
evolving with time

834

each soul's unique road
nonlinear odyssey
in search of Divine

835

man hides in shadows
Jesus draws near veil removed
truth seen in his gaze

836

offering his hands
no need for wallet's hiding
truth lies in the heart

837

on a weathered porch
a hundred birds take to flight
cat's eyes watch unmoved

838

wings beat through still air
sky echoes with memory
life's pulse resonates

839

each one plays its part
cosmic symphony unfolds
fleeting harmony

840

in dim lit corner
weary soul clutches his bag
automat's shadows

841

ten cents buys black brew
buttered rolls for calloused hands
waiting for the dawn

842

rough fingers seek change
flies buzz on stained cups dull forks
life's harshness displayed

843

green tape on red seats
cracked vinyl and weary bones
silent lament fills

844

chipped cups greasy plates
toothless mouths chew tasteless beans
stories in whispers

845

love's terrain stretches
bridges built on trust's foundation
hearts learning to mend

846

to cross divides wide
mapping inner fears with care
trust builds the pathway

847

connection's true form
found in love's struggle and strain
striving hearts unite

848

no fear in shadows
your rod and staff my comfort
valleys hold no dread

849

your gaze dissects me
cutting to my core exposed
laid bare in your sight

850

flesh peeled back wounds deep
pain's sharpness finds no solace
hearts bleed sutured closed

851

suctioned and sealed tight
but silence speaks louder still
life fades to ashes


852

faith my anchor strong
amid stormy seas I trust
patience by my side


853

eyes fixed on hope's light
burdens eased by mercy's grace
faith leads me through storms


854

small dark eyes shiver
hidden beneath shaggy mane
fear in trembling heart


855

afraid to touch stillness
pain stirs quietly within
a soul waits alone

856

dry earth splits open
even without the promise
of rain roots reach down

857

hot sun stillness sand
faith waits like an empty hand
under endless skies

858

no peaks no valleys
just the long stretch of nothing
shadow trips on dust

859

wind without a voice
sweeps dunes of forgotten steps
God moves unseen here

860

the old sage whispers
God is where you least expect
underneath silence

861

keep walking they say
though sand looks only like sand
the path finds itself

862

maybe it's enough
to stumble over nothing
to hear your own breath

863

even doubts crackle
even thirst speaks demanding
what's left what's beyond

864

faith is walking blind
in a land with no border
where shadows don't cling

865

this is where God hides
in the grit between each breath
where silence answers

866

truth never spoke twice
dusty tongues of prophets drowned
priests' leatherbound growls

867

slick words of the wise
bounced off walls of coffee shops
echoed into smoke

868

it never knocked once
on your door that bleeding beast
homeless truth prefers

869

a stranger's laugh
or the glance from your mother
when she thought you didn't see

870

truth crawls under skin
when the dog barks at nothing
wind rattling windows

871

it's a stray mutt's bark
in a hundred accents lost
in the night's silence


872

we begged for one truth
to fit in our pockets small
to tell us it all


873

but real truth is this
bones aching in different ways
smoke you can't quite grasp


874

one word never learned
in all the world's dictionaries
something almost said


875

if it had one tongue
we'd miss it like a dance step
out of time off beat

876

static on the road
cutting through the desert sand
song with no music

877

so truth shatters down
into shards that bleed us dry
just enough to hurt

878

mystic hears angels
scientist echoes of space
poet blames the moon

879

all right all of them
wrong just a stray alley cat
never lets you close

880

sun rises again
even when the world should stop
no one dares protest

881

and that's where it hides
in coffee cups' cooled silence
hymns with no meaning

882

half heard curses tossed
into empty winds lost notes
faint slipping away

883

primordial truth
never a single clear voice
a scream in the dark

884

child of chaos born
to a world split black and white
that dreams only hues

885

just its shadow here
brushing past like a whisper
almost recognized

886

everything it says
in every language ends up
nothing for no one


887

the universe hums
to itself a soft murmur
alone in the void


888

Christ's light marks the path
soul reaching breaking its chains
truth piercing through doubt


889

sharp words cut through fog
of fear a bright steady beam
calm amid the noise


890

truth buried below
hidden pure as an old stone
calls those who dare dig

891

the road twists shadowed
His light shreds darkness apart
revealing freedom

892

in grace we let go
weights of shame fall step by step
lightness in each stride

893

life stripped down to love
bare and clear we walk in light
breathing in pure grace

894

sun breaks through cloud gaps
light spills like grace on still fields
shadowed hearts unfold

895

spring rain on dry earth
God's voice heard in the silence
roots drink deeply in

896

cross-shaped bird shadow
glides on the water's surface
flesh and spirit merge

897

ancient oak branches
wind hums the psalms of angels
lost in green silence

898

stop trying to fit
truth into a small glass jar
dust settles inside

899

all those voices speak
like hands grasping at thick fog
each tongue grabbing air

900

one note never sung
each song breaks off mid-silence
lost in empty noise

901

call it Absolute
dress it up in bright black words
it won't wear your name

902

call it One it splits
in half before you can blink
like light through stained glass

903

the Absolute fades
a ghost at the eye's corner
gone when you turn back

904

not just formlessness
each shape a mask on nothing
each mask a bright lie

905

all words carve it up
like slicing through empty space
still nothing bleeds out

906

what is just remains
not something you can label
not pinned to your maps

907

every prayer a line
each chant a circle drawn 'round
something too bright lost

908

no root no clear branch
all these tangled forms reaching
from groundless ground

909

every belief smoke
a different cut of clear glass
fracturing the light

910

step back do not chase
don't cut it down to pieces
silence knows its place

911

searching shapes the void
with shadows of our own words
let the silence speak


912

the Absolute waits
indifferent to knowing
it just is and stays


913

the shape you gave it
was never its own but yours
let it slip through hands


914

put down the scissors
let silence grow stretching out
listen to the space


915

in stillness grace breathes
a sparrow's wingbeat over
the hushed forest pond

916

sins dissolve like fog
lifting from wet fields at dawn
grass sighs dew glistens

917

soul finds quiet rest
where the cattail bends softly
to the river's song

918

cicada voices
sins left clinging to branches
forgotten shed skins

919

a moth on closed palms
rests its stillness becomes mine
no flight no flutter

920

the old crow watches
black eyes like polished onyx
under morning's veil

921

sins like cobweb strands
stretch sway but they do not stick
to hands that stay still


922

no judgment here no
condemnation in the moss
or in the cloud's gaze


923

each fallen leaf sighs
this too shall pass on its way
to rejoin the earth


924

in quiet a breeze
whispers through unseen fingers
touching then moving


925

no sermons no shouts
the forest forgives in sighs
the river absolves

926

sins sharp-edged pebbles
tossed into the lake's mirror
ripples swallow all

927

rest in still water
see the fish flash through darkness
one with what it swims

928

stones drop to the ground
no one counts them no one speaks
their weight their value

929

a single leaf falls
without a name no guilt no
blame just one leaf's fall

930

the sparrow returns
pecking seeds in cool silence
as if nothing's changed

931

no confession made
except breath drawn and released
grace comes with each sigh

932

moon above the pine
sees all and says nothing more
than silver-white light

933

the night forgives all
and when dawn comes there's nothing
left to cast shadows

934

sin like mist has gone
where it cannot be measured
where light pierces through

935

in stillness grace breathes
like a prayer never spoken
the heart's beat is calm

936

hands empty palms wide
open to the sky's silence
held without asking

937

sins what were they now
just echoes just loosened dreams
caught up in bird flight

938

stillness remains still
forgiveness is just letting
mist rise to the sun

939

let my faith stumble
vision blur truth waits in shade
quiet desert breeze

940

twilight's soft descent
world fades real things rise slowly
night's hidden secrets

941

ancient winds whisper
secrets borne by desert sands
silence leans to hear

942

as light dies I see
not with eyes but something deep
glowing in the dark

943

in uncertainty
shadows dance Divine hum sings
what words cannot hold

944

desert breeze cool touch
takes my doubts away like dust
something endless breathes

945

faith falters sight dims
giving up knowing reveals
heart of all wisdom

946

silence through dry sands
teaches light was always there
waiting for stillness

947

in failing I see
a seeing beyond seeing
truth without answers

948

in shadows night's hum
brings wisdom not in knowing
only in release

949

no one gets out clean
gold road or dirt same damn end
bones beneath each step

950

call it sacred truth
call it destiny's bright lie
we trip in the dark

951

sky never looks down
we stumble on shoes worn thin
storm without a map

952

preachers yell for grace
poets drown in empty dreams
dust chokes every hymn

953

move forward or die
backwards just leads to more hell
no compass for this

954

call it survival
no gods just broken bodies
and bruises we hide

955

I crawl alleys deep
built by my own hands seeking
something like your love

956

roads twist through gutters
shadows play where light won't go
my soul bent and torn

957

at dawn's break your voice
pulls me down the cracked asphalt
heartbeat in the dark

958

fields of doubt fear's grip
faith flickers wet match burning
through a starless night

959

when silence settles
your breath soft as a friend's hand
finds me in the noise

960

teach me to let go
a cracked vase that still holds rain
light in broken glass

961

each breath each heartbeat
make me a mirror of you
truth raw as bare stone

962

the road's long dim-lit
but your love unending sky
keeps me crawling on

963

hold me in this time
let my jagged life become
a song sung for you

964

the Lord is one thread
holding loose ends of the world
quilt of night and day

965

chaos calm entwined
stitched in quiet breaths of faith
whole despite the gaps

966

needle through soft cloth
the hands of God sew dark light
one pattern unseen

967

tangled lines and knots
each piece finds place in the quilt
one touch weaves them all

968

patchwork sky above
each star stitched to hold the night
whole in broken light

969

the Lord is one wind
through the pine branches whisper
that holds all as one

970

love with all your heart
each beat a prayer to mend cracks
moon in shattered pond

971

love with all your soul
ghost-light on the path at dusk
faint yet still shining

972

love with all your mind
maze of thought leads to clear sky
stars no questions asked

973

love with all your strength
even when bones bend and break
still lean into love

974

fragments of the world
split glass caught in morning sun
one light many shapes

975

heart as battlefield
mind like fog yet still I walk
the path of wholeness

976

Lord is one they say
and I a torn cloth threadbare
search for that one thread

977

step by step I go
trying to love what is whole
in what's cracked and split

978

Lord is one soft wind
through a maze of broken reeds
tangled into grace

979

bar full of lost souls
her neck smooth as pink tomato
nature's elegance

980

cigarette smoke hangs
voices blend into dull noise
all I see is her

981

soft curve delicate
like something untouched by grime
a slice of heaven

982

graceful that small truth
quiet in a loud rough place
beauty's whispering

983

even here this bar
her neck soft against the dark
world's edge fades away

984

nature got it right
a reminder even now
there's still light somewhere

985

I sit stare and breathe
ugliness slips for a while
as she holds that grace

986

lovely lady's neck
curved like some small piece of peace
gentle in the mess

987

graceful tomato
a strange thing to find right here
amid all that's wrong

988

yet for this moment
that softness quiets my mind
a world gone quiet

989

I sip and I watch
how sometimes just sometimes
life gets beauty right

990

chasm stretches wide
emptiness between two hearts
echoes of lost thoughts

991

mind seeks a strong bridge
to span the clouds of doubt's mist
beyond what words fail

992

trust connects like thread
hearts rediscover old warmth
familiar touch's grace

993

stumbling through darkness
reaching for that fragile line
back to warmth again

994

chaos of two lives
a delicate dance of love
each step a new plea

995

to be seen and known
held in mutual light's glow
truth in recognition

996

tangled webs of fear
searching for one clear moment
truth in silent storms

997

we build with our words
each honest plank laid with care
hope's bridge takes its shape

998

silent spaces speak
love whispers where words break down
truth breathes in still air

999

in vast empty lands
we stumble rise fall as one
hands clasped in the dark

1000

moving toward the light
small flicker on the far edge
faith across the void

1001

love's barren terrain
stretching far and wide ahead
we build step by step

1002

with courage to face
the empty expanse of fear
and faith to cross it

1003

emptiness so wide
echo of doubt's hollow sound
hearts call out alone

1004

we reach through the void
hands searching for something close
something warm to hold

1005

mind builds fragile bridge
hopes it spans this lonely gap
but words often fail

1006

trust a thin thread pulled
two hearts meet like old friends lost
finding warmth again

1007

stumble through shadows
grasping for that line of light
past the edge of fear

1008

each step through silence
love's dance on uncertain ground
soft plea to be seen

1009

tangled thoughts like weeds
searching for a clear path through
truth in tangled threads

1010

we build plank by plank
with each act of kindness shown
bridge across the dark

1011

in silent spaces
unspoken truths softly hum
where whispers reside


1012

hands build what words can't
hope stretches between the cracks
breath by breath we cross


1013

in the vast unknown
we stumble and rise as one
always moving on


1014

love's terrain so wide
as we build in faith and trust
step by step we reach


1015

through fear's empty land
hands clasped in a quiet vow
to find light again

1016

holy elixir
blood of Christ in the wine glass
transfiguration


1017

bite into muffin
dark alleys whisper softly
lovers kiss then part


1018

sleepless nights bring change
wrapped tight in lies and old truths
waiting for the crack


1019

when we shed old skin
wings glisten in morning light
raw and new again


1020

life's chisel at work
reveals rough edges and gold
hidden in the stone

1021

growing through the grime
to find who we truly are
essence beneath flesh

1022

dust settles at last
Christ's hands pour the last of wine
we stand spirit new

1023

lifting cups in thanks
to the Spirit of great change
to ghosts of our past

1024

in quiet moments
we see strangers in mirrors
no more what we were

1025

sum of all trials
each loss a stroke of the brush
a note in life's song

1026

streets like galleries
each step paints a masterpiece
truth shines through the dark

1027

through smoke and shadows
emerging bruised but unbroken
wounded yet wiser

1028

we cannot remain
for each breath shapes us anew
something real takes form

1029

life's journey unfolds
we are sculptor and the stone
changing as we carve

1030

flick of a match's spark
sunlight on morning sidewalks
golden light whispers

1031

bad egg in the pan
sizzling with sour regret
maybe the hen's fault

1032

clothes on thin bodies
etched faces stare through the night
regrets woven deep

1033

fingers trace glass rims
redemption in the dark drink
neon hums softly

1034

a ghost hovers near
forgiveness slips like the wind
just out of their reach

1035

Jesus takes a sip
thunder grumbles in the clouds
grief pours through the room

1036

tired eyes glance upward
indifferent weary gaze
shared in silent knowing

1037

eucharist dissolves
Christ's blood flows in quiet streams
through my trembling veins

1038

digging through the muck
past chatter and empty noise
to the raw bare soul

1039

been down this road once
stripping lies like old chipped paint
truth doesn't flinch back

1040

good and evil fade
a shadow dance a soft blur
none of it sticks here

1041

deep in that dark corner
where the real self quietly hides
nothing else matters

1042

no saints no sinners
just a heartbeat in the void
laughing at the gods

1043

freedom in emptiness
shedding the world's heavy weight
like a worn-out coat

1044

just you in the mess
bare and honest standing still
maybe that's enough

1045

black moths glide softly
moonflower opens its heart
night whispers secrets

1046

golden blades sway high
reaching for the endless sky
nature's gentle touch

1047

eagles circle wide
wings tracing the summer breeze
freedom on the wing

1048

deep blue water shines
reflecting all the quiet
stillness in the depths

1049

under moonlit skies
life weaves through shadows and light
the world breathes as one

1050

broken wires no light
toaster spits sparks in the dark
kitchen full of ghosts

1051

fridge grinds like old bones
no bulbs to fix anything
silent stubborn night

1052

screwdriver's buried
in the basement's dusty maze
lost with failed projects

1053

hell if I'll go down
not tonight not in this dark
let it stay broken

1054

cat sits smug and still
smirking at me in the gloom
perfectly content

1055

he's got me pegged right
just watching me chase shadows
a man without hope

1056

pisses on the wall
then leaps onto the made bed
victory complete

1057

maybe I'll join him
leave the mess and tangled wires
dream of toast and light

1058

let the dark conquer
cat keep his throne in the night
some battles aren't mine

1059

stay in bed forget
shadows can have the kitchen
I'm not fighting them

1060

cat and I are same
chasing ghosts and sleeping in
waiting for the dawn

1061

you who breathe star dust
into the quiet of nightfall
and paint first daylight

1062

we are cracked vessels
aching for your gentle touch
lost in the dark fields

1063

yet you are the breeze
that stirs the sleeping leaves still
and calls us to peace

1064

teach us to listen
in newborn cries and still breath
the silence speaks loud

1065

plant your word in us
let mercy bloom from dry lands
hope where none remains

1066

we lay down our wounds
and offer prayers like petals
trusting they will float


1067

in this brokenness
let us feel your presence near
love folded in peace


1068

hide in the still dark
where no one can see your light
whisper your soft prayers


1069

walls press hard around
thick clay that holds like the grave
you breathe in black seas


1070

memories wrap tight
like a second skin that bites
and soothes with each touch

1071

on faraway hills
you sing blessings to the wind
no stars hear your song

1072

every scar exposed
yet somehow you still remain
breathing free at last

1073

Jesus walks inside
pulls you deep into the cave
flips you inside out

1074

Jesus leads you up
lets you taste the light then hands
you the weight to bear

1075

Jesus reminds you
the path you walk is his own
glory and the cross

Printed in the United States
by Baker & Taylor Publisher Services